ISBN 978-1-333-60180-5
PIBN 10524997

1 MONTH OF
FREE
READING

at
www.ForgottenBooks.com

By purchasing this book you are eligible for one month membership to ForgottenBooks.com, giving you unlimited access to our entire collection of over 700,000 titles via our web site and mobile apps.

To claim your free month visit:
www.forgottenbooks.com/free524997

English
Français
Deutsche
Italiano
Español
Português

www.forgottenbooks.com

Mythology Photography **Fiction**
Fishing Christianity **Art** Cooking
Essays Buddhism Freemasonry
Medicine **Biology** Music **Ancient
Egypt** Evolution Carpentry Physics
Dance Geology **Mathematics** Fitness
Shakespeare **Folklore** Yoga Marketing
Confidence Immortality Biographies
Poetry **Psychology** Witchcraft
Electronics Chemistry History **Law**
Accounting **Philosophy** Anthropology
Alchemy Drama Quantum Mechanics
Atheism Sexual Health **Ancient History**
Entrepreneurship Languages Sport
Paleontology Needlework Islam
Metaphysics Investment Archaeology
Parenting Statistics Criminology
Motivational

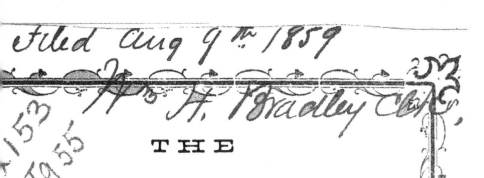

THE

E'OPLE'S FRIEND

A NEW AND VALUABLE

COMPENDIUM

OF

SCELLANEOUS & DOMESTIC

NY OF WHICH ARE OF INCALCULABLE VALUE, AND WHICH ARE NOW PUBLISHED FOR THE FIRST TIME.

Selected, Compiled and Carefully Revised by

WM. F. TUTHILL.

GALESBURG, ILL.:

2 1 846

THE

PEOPLE'S FRIEND

A NEW AND VALUABLE

COMPENDIUM

OF

MISCELLANEOUS & DOMESTIC

MANY OF WHICH ARE OF INCALCULABLE
VALUE, AND WHICH ARE NOW PUB-
LISHED FOR THE FIRST TIME.

Selected, Compiled and Carefully Revised by

WM. F. TUTHILL.

Copyright Secured according to Law.

GALESBURG, ILL. :

BEN FRANKLIN PRINTING HOUSE.

1859.

TABLE OF WEIGHT AND MEASURE.

To remedy a difficulty that has heretofore existed in works of this character, the quantity of ingredients used being generally given in weight, we subjoin the following valuable Table of Weight and Measure. It is necessary to observe, however, that due allowance must be made for quality, dryness, moisture, etc., of the articles used.

An ounce of cinnamon, ginger, pepper, spice, or cloves, two large table-spoonfuls.

RECEIPTS.

SPIRIT SOAP.

For removing paint, grease, etc., from Woolen Goods.

Take 95 per cent. Alcohol,....2 quarts.
"   Aq. Ammonia,...........1 quart.
"   1 oz. of Salæratus dis. in 1 qt. Soft water.
"   Cologne Water,....... 4 oz.

Fit for use, immediately. Apply with sponge, and rinse with water.

A VALUABLE RECEIPT

For CLEANSING and RESTORING COLOR to Soiled or Faded Coats, Vests, Pants and Woollen Goods of every description.

THIS RECEIPT HAS BEEN SOLD FOR $50.00.

Place the article to be cleansed on a table and carefully brush all dust and dirt from it; then with a sponge apply the Spirit Soap which will completely remove all spots of paint, grease, tar, etc. Then with a sponge wet the garment thoroughly with boiling soft water into which some yellow bar soap has been dissolved. Then apply, immediately, the following preparation to restore the color:

For dark colors, take ½ pint Logwood chips, put into one pailful soft water and heat on fire until the strength or color is out of the chips. Add, to set the color, a piece of blue Vitriol size of a small walnut, and the same amount of Coperas, also ¼ ounce Gum Arabic. Apply boiling hot with a brush, and hang up in the shade to dry—occasionally brushing it, always with the napp, until dry. For drab or light colors omit the logwood.

TO SUGAR CURE BEEF.

To every 100 lbs beef, 10 lbs salt, 4 lbs brown sugar (moistened with water) or 3 pints molasses, mix the above ingredients together and rub the pieces beef, and pack it down in a barrel, let it stand 2 or 3 days then make a brine and pour on your meat enough to cover it.

JET BLACK WRITING INK.

To 1 gallon boiling soft water, add 1½ oz. of ex. Logwood, stir till dissolved ; then one tenth oz. Bicarbonate of Potash, and one tenth oz. Prussiate Potash. Stir till cool.

INDELIBLE INK.

Take 60 grs. Lunar Caustic, (Nitrate of Silver,) mix with one oz. Soft Water. Pour ¼ gill boiling water upon one drachm powdered Nut Gall, and add 18 drops of the liquid to the Nitrate of Silver.

For preparation to apply to the cloth before marking with the above, take ½ gill of water and dissolve as much salæratus as it will hold in solution, and add 5 grains of Gum Arabic. After marking, the fabric should be exposed to the sun.

PHŒNIX LINIMENT.

Take one pound of fresh butter and heat and skim until all impurities are removed. Then cool a little and add 2 ozs. Oil of Origanum and one spoonful of Spirits of Turpentine, well mixed.

WHITEWASH FOR FENCES AND OUT HOUSES.

Unslaked lime, one bushel; salt one peck 3 lbs. ground rice, powdered whiting 2 lbs glue (dissolved) 1 lb. Slake the lime in boiling water in a covered vessel strain through a wire seive, add the salt dissolved in hot water, add, while hot, the rice boiled to a thin paste, then the glue and whiting, let stand several days, put it on hot.

WASHING & BLEACHING LIQUID.

Take ¼ ℔. unslaked lime, and pour upon it 6 qts. boiling water, stir it all up, and when it has stood long enough to entirely settle, strain off the clear water and dissolve in this water, by boiling 2 ℔s. sal soda.

For washing—to every pail full of water add while boiling, ½ pint of the liquid. The clothes must be put in soak the night before washing, taking care to rub all the dirt spots with soap; then boil them with the liquid 35 minutes. They are then to be drawn and put into a tub, and clear boiling water poured on them; then rub them out rinse them well and they are fit for drying.

TO KEEP PORK SWEET AS WHEN FIRST SALTED.

After your meat is entirely cold pack it down in a cask or barrel with plenty coarse salt, then make a strong brine and pour it on the meat boiling hot; be sure and have your meat covered with brine.

WHITEWASH THAT WILL NOT RUB OFF.

Mix up half a pailful of lime take a half pint of flour and make it into starch, pour into the whitewash while hot stir it well and it is ready for use.

ITALIAN SOAP.

For removing Grease and Stains from Fancy Colored
SILKS, etc without injury to the fabric.

Take of Beef's Gall......1 ℔
"   Castile Soap,........1 ℔
"   Starch, one spoonful.
"   Camomile flowers, one handful.

Melt Gall and Soap together, and add juice of Camomile flowers after steeping, also add Starch, while hot, and it will be fit for use as soon as cold.

For Woollen Goods add 2 oz. Spirits of Turpentine, and 1 oz. Cream Tartar, to the above.

GOOD SAMARITAN LINIMENT.

Take Lobelia Herb ....2 ozs.
"   Annies Flowers, ...2 ozs.
"   Capicum,............2 ozs.
"   Alcohol 4th. proof,....3 quarts.

Macerate the above 14 days, and strain.

LIFE LINIMENT.

Take Lard,................1 ℔.
"   Flowers of Benzoin,.....2 drachms.
"   Oil Bergamot,.........1   "
"   Oil Sassafras,.........1   "
"   Beeswax,.............4 ozs.
"   Resin,................1 oz.
"   Sugar Lead,..........½ oz.
"   Oil Anise,............1 drachm.

TO DESTROY COCKROACHES, RATS AND MICE.

Take a sixpenny loaf of bread, the staler the better, reduce it to a crumb, then in a pot of water put two spoonfuls cayenne pepper, one do. pulverised annise seed, half a drachm of saltpetre, the same of white lead, and a wine glass of extract of hops. Now throw in your crumbs of bread; digest for six hours in a moderate heat; strain through a cloth; add to the liquor thirty drops of the tincture of quassia, and let it stand until next day, and then bottle it. Some lumps of sugar saturated with this liquor will be a speedy cure for cockroaches. Some pieces of bread saturated with it, will destroy all the rats and mice. The above is extensively manufactured and sold at a great profit.

PRESERVING EGGS FOR WINTER.

Take new laid eggs, have ready melted Lard and with a skimmer dip the Eggs in and pack them in a box or keg with small ends downward and set them in a cool place. The Lard stops the pores of the shell and thus excludes the air; by resting on the small end the yelk is prevented from reaching the shell.

Domestic Receipts.

FRUIT CAKE.

Two lbs butter, two of sugar, two of flour, two doz eggs, three lbs currants six lbs raisins, 1¾ lb citron, ½ oz nutmeg, 1 table spoonful ginger, ½ pint brandy, a little saleratus.

BLACK PLUM CAKE.

Take 1 lb Flour, 1 ℔ Sugar, 1 ℔ Butter, 8 Eggs, one glass of Wine, one glass of Brandy, 6 ℔s fruit, including citron and spices. Brown the flour.

FANCY CAKE.

4 cups flour, 3 of sugar, 1 of milk, 1 of butter, 5 eggs, 2 teaspoons pearlash, fruit to your taste.

CREAM CAKE.

5 eggs, 3 cups sugar 1 cup of butter, 4 of flour, 1 cup of cream, 1 tea-spoon saleratus.

COMMON TEA CAKES.

½ pint new milk, ½ lb sugar, ¼ lb butter,

GOOD SPONGE CAKE.

Beat together the yelks of ten eggs with 1 lb of white sugar, beat to a stiff froth the eggs and stir them into the yelks and the sugar, beat the whole ten or fifteen minutes, stir ¾ of a lb sifted flour, flavor with a nutmeg or the rind of a lemon; bake as soon as well mixed.

CAROLINA CAKE.

1 coffee cup of sugar, ½ cup cream, 1 of flour, whites of 4 eggs, 1 table-spoon of butter, and part of a nutmeg.

TEA CAKES.

1 cup of butter, 2 of sugar, 2 eggs, 1 teaspoon of saleratus dissolved in a tea-cup of sour milk or cream, flour sufficient to stiffen so as to roll out well.

COMPOSITION CAKE.

1 cup butter, 1 of milk, 2½ of sugar, 4 eggs, 1 tea-spoon saleratus, flour to make it stiff as pound cake, spice to your taste.

FRUIT CAKE.

6 eggs, 1½ coffee cups molasses, 2 of sugar, 1 pint sour milk, saleratus, 1 tea-cup of butter, 2 lbs raisins, cloves and currants.

CORN CAKE.

The whites of 8 eggs ¼ lb corn starch, flour, butter, ½ lb sugar, 1 teaspoon cream-tartar, ½ of soda, flavor with almonds, or to suit the taste.

POUND CAKE.

Take 1 ℔ Flour, 1 lb Sugar, 14 oz. Butter, 1 lb Eggs; Lemon and Nutmeg.

ANOTHER.

Take one pound flour, one pound sugar, ¾ lb butter, 6 eggs, one cup sour cream, one tea spoon Salæratus.

ANOTHER.

Take one cup butter, two cups sugar, four eggs, and a very little sweet milk, and one lb. of flour.

GINGER CAKE.

1 cup Molasses, 1 cup sour milk, with 1 tea spoon full of soda in each, beat them well together, and add ⅔ cup of butter, 1 table spoon ginger, and 3 cups flour.

CIDER CAKE.

Three cups flour, 2 cups sugar, 1½ lb. butter, 2 eggs, 1 cup cider with a teaspoon pearlash dissolved in it; the pearlash and cider to be added when ready to go into the oven.

PLUM PUDDING.

12 Crackers, 3 half pints of Milk, 8 Eggs, 4 table spoonsful Flour, 1 ℔ Raisins, 1 ℔ Currants, ¾ ℔ Suet, 6 Apples, 1 Nutmeg, 2 glasses Wine, 1 tea cup brown Sugar, a piece of Butter size of a walnut, a few thin slices of Citron.

Roll the Crackers fine and pour the milk over them boiling hot. After cooling beat the eggs in well with them, and add the other ingredients.

Boil 5 hours. Scald the cloth and flour it well. Half this quantity will make a good sized pudding. Put into boiling water.

TRANSPARENT PUDDING.

Take 8 Eggs, beat them well, white and yelks separately; put them in a pan, add ½ ℔ finely powdered Sugar and half a nutmeg. Set it over a chafing dish of coals, and stir it for some time; then set it away to cool.

Put a thin puff paste around the edge of a dish, pour in the ingredients, bake it half an hour in a gentle oven, and serve it hot or cold.

WHITE POUND CAKE.

Two cups butter, two cups cream, 2¼ cups sugar, whites of ten eggs, 3½ cups flour, a little salæratus.

LEMON PUDDING.

1 ℔ Sugar, 10 Eggs, ½ ℔ Butter, grated rind of two Lemons, juice of one Lemon, one glass of Wine, one glass of Rose water.

Cream the butter, add the sugar, then add the eggs after beating the white and yelks separately. It should be well beaten when all together.

Bake in a deep dish with puff paste under it.

POTATO PUDDING.

Take 1 lb Potatoes, peel and boil them, ½ lb Butter, ¾ lb Sugar, 1 coffee cup of Cream 1 coffee cup of Wine, 1 Nutmeg, 1 teaspoon of Mace, and 6 Eggs.

Beat the potatoes well, by degrees put in a little butter until you mix it all; then add the sugar, beat the eggs very light, then add all together with the grated rind and juice of one lemon.

Make a puff paste on a plate and put the pudding on. Bake in a gentle oven.

TROY HOUSE CORN CAKE.

3 large cups Indian meal, ½ of flour, 1 qt. sour milk, 1 eggs, ½ tea-spoon salt, ½ tea-spoon soda, beat well together, bake one quarter of an hour.

RIPE CUCUMBER PICKLES.

Pare the Cucumbers and cut them into thin slices. Then put them in a jar and cover them with Cider Vinegar, let them stand 24 hours, then pour off the Vinegar and make a syrup of it.

To one gallon of Vinegar add 4 lbs. Sugar, and Spices to the taste.

Boil the Syrup and cook the Cucumbers in it until they are a little tender. Then boil the Syrup down for half an hour, and pour it hot upon the Cucumbers. Fit for use when cold.

For spices use to every gallon
2 table spoonful Cloves.
1 " " Allspice.
1 " " Mace.
1½ ozs. Cinnamon.

PICKLED PEACHES.

One quart Cider Vinegar, 4 lbs. Brown Sugar. Boil for a few minutes and skim off impurities. Rub off the down and stick three or four cloves into each peach.

Place them in a jar and pour the liquor over them boiling hot.

Cover and let them stand a week or ten days. Then pour off the liquor, and boil it as before.

Return it boiling hot and cover them.

GREEN TOMATO PICKLE.

One bushel tomatoes 1 qt. green peppers, 1 qt. of grated horseraddish, 1 cup of white mustard, ground; 1½ grated lemons, 8 onions. Chop fine the tomatoes and onions and put them in a vessel over night with a layer of salt and tomatoes. The next morning drain and scald them in vinegar till tender, drain, pack in jars, cover in vinegar.

PICKLED CUCUMBERS.

Make a brine to bear up an egg, and pour it over your pickles boiling hot. Let them stand 24 hours; then take them out, wipe them with dry cloth and put them in cold vinegar.

To every gallon vinegar add—

Cloves, a table spoon full.
Allspice, 2   "
Mace, ½   "
Mustard, 1   "

One piece ginger root, a lump of Alum size of a walnut, two green peppers, and let the whole come to a scald, BUT NOT BOIL, and then put in jars.

DELIA'S CAKE.

2 cups sugar, 1 of butter, 3 of flour, 4 eggs ½ cup of milk, ¼ tea-spoon soda in the flour, 1 of cream-tartar, milk flavor to taste.

SUET PUDDING.

2 quarts milk, ½ lb suet, boil the milk and stir in the suet (chopped fine) and 1 pint sifted Indian meal and a little salt, let it stand till cold, add 2 eggs, 1 table-spoon flour 1 tea-cup bro. sugar and sweeten to taste with molasses, and add 1 tablespoonful ginger, and 1 lb raisins, put in dish to bake and grate nutmeg over it.

When about half baked and well browned throw 2 or 3 spoonfuls of milk over it to make it whey.

GREEN CORN PUDDING.

Take of green corn twelve ears, grate it to this add one quart of sweet milk, ¼ lb of fresh butter, 4 eggs well beaten, pepper, and salt to taste, stir all together, and bake it hours in a buttered dish.

Some add ¼ lb sugar and eat the pudding with sauce, it is good cold or warm with meat or sauce.

CHARLOTT DE RUSE.

1½ pints milk, 6 eggs to make soft custard, 1 oz. ising-glass dissolved and mixed with the custard, let it cool, then whip a quart of cream and add it to the custard, put it in your dish lined with sponge cake and sit it in a cool place to form.

LEMON PIE.

Take one lemon and a half, cut them up fine, one cup of molasses, half cup of sugar, two eggs; mix them together, prepare your plate, with a crust in the bottom; put in half the materials, lay over a crust, then put in the rest of the materials, and cover the whole with another crust.

MINCE PIES.

Take 4 ℔s Meat, 6 ℔s Apples, ¾ ℔ Suet, 2 fresh Lemons, a little Wine, a little Brandy, and Cider enough to make it sufficiently wet. Cloves, Cinnamon, Fruit and Sugar to your taste.

Pack it down in a stone jar, cover it closely and it will keep good during the winter, if kept in a cold place.

CUSTARD PIE.

Take one pint milk, half a pint of cream, three eggs, 3 table spoons sugar, and a little salt.

DOUGH NUTS.

Set a sponge with 1 pint of milk, and when light, add 4 boiled mashed potatoes, 6 ozs. Sugar, and 6 ozs. Butter.

Set to raise, and when light, roll out and fry.

CORN OYSTERS.

Take 3 dozen ears of corn, 6 eggs, lard and butter in equal proportions, for frying take young corn and grate from cob as fine as possible and drege it with wheat flour. Beat very light the eggs and mix gradually with the corn, then beat the whole hard, add salt; put butter and lard over the fire heat hot, and then put in the mixture with spoon so as to form cool cakes three inches long and an inch thick fry brown and eat hot.

BLACK PUDDING OR DELIA'S WASHINGTON PUDDING.

8 eggs, $\frac{1}{2}$ cup butter, 1 of sugar, 1 of milk 1 of flour, 1 tea-spoon soda, to be baked.

DELIA'S PLUM PUDDING.

$\frac{1}{2}$ lb suet, 1 of bread, 1 large cup molasses, $\frac{1}{2}$ lb raisins, $\frac{1}{2}$ of currants, a spoonful of flour, boil 3 hours.

LEMON PIE.

Take one lemon, one coffee cup sugar, one coffee cup water, three small crackers, and one egg.

DUTCH WOFFLES.

3 eggs, 1 quart milk, $\frac{3}{4}$ lb butter, add yeast sufficient to raise them.

SOFT GINGERBREAD.

Three teacups molasses, 1 cup of butter, 4 eggs, ½ cup sour cream, or milk, nearly a teaspoon of pearlash dissolved in a little warm water. Flour enough to make it as stiff as pound cake.

GINGER NUTS.

Rub 1 ℔ butter in 3 ℔s flour, 1 ℔ sugar, 2 oz. ginger, a large nutmeg, grated, ½ pint molasses, a gill cream, 1 teaspoon full pearlash. Make them all warm together—roll them.

GINGER NUTS.

One pound butter, 1 ℔ sugar, 2 cups molasses, 1 oz. ginger. Flour sufficient to roll them.

SPONGE GINGER CAKE.

1 pint of molasses, ½ of sweet milk, 2 of flour, 1 table-spoon vinegar, 1 of soda, 1 of ginger, 2 of butter.

ORANGE PUDDING.

Take 1 ℔ Butter, 1 ℔ Sugar, 10 Eggs, the rind of a sweet Orange, the juice of half a Lemon, and a glass of Wine and Rosewater.

QUEEN'S CAKE

One pound flour, 1 ℔ sugar, ¾ ℔ butter, 5 eggs, 1½ oz. nutmeg, 1 gill brandy, 1 gill wine, 1 gill cream, 1 ℔ raisins.

Put the brandy, wine, cream and nutmeg together, let them simmer and mix well, then add them to the butter and sugar, after beating them together, then add the eggs, well beaten, then the flour. It should be put in the oven immediately after the flour is put in.

OLICOOKS.

Six eggs, 1 quart milk, ¾ ℔ sugar, ¾ lb butter, beat them together with as much flour as you can STIR into them, add yeast enough to raise them; when light, put them in a cold place. Before frying, add cinnamon or nutmeg to your taste.

DOUGH NUTS.

One cup butter, 2 cups sugar, 4 cups of milk, yeast sufficient to raise them.

SODA FRIED CAKES.

1 qt. Flour, One Egg.
Three table spoonfuls Sugar, ½ pt. sweet milk, 3 teaspoons Cream Tartar in the milk, 1 spoon soda in the flour, 2 table spoons butter. Spice to taste.

COCOA-NUT JUMBLES.

Grate a large cocoa-nut, rub a half pound of butter into one pound of sifted flour, and wet it with three beaten eggs and a little rosewater; add by degrees the cocoa-nut so as to form a stiff paste or dough. Flour your hands and paste board; divide your dough into equal portions. Make the jumblers into rings; grate loaf sugar over them, put into buttered pans, (not so near as to run into each other,) and bake in a quick oven from 5 to 10 minutes.

GINGER NUTS.

One and a half cup of butter one of sugar two cups of molasses table spoonfull of ginger cloves cinnamon &c. and as much flour as can easily be worked in, roll this and cut them small and round.

TO CURE CORNS.

A writer in one of the agricultural papers declares on his own experience, that to pare corns and then apply a drop or two of wormwood oil, is a certain cure.

JUMBLES.

1¼ pounds flour, 1 of sugar, ½ of butter, 3 eggs, and nutmeg,

SAUSAGES.

To 10 lbs of meat chopped fine, add 4 oz. salt, 1 oz. pepper and 1 oz. of sage, moisten the above with a little warm water, and make into ball or as you like.

DROP CAKE.

1 gallon molasses, 2 lbs lard, 2 ozs. ginger, $\frac{1}{2}$ lb saleratus, flour, enough to make it stiff enough to work.

GINGER CORDIAL.

Four pounds Red Currants, (or White,)
8 ozs. Jamaica Ginger Root, bruised,
2 " Bitter Almonds, "
1 " Sweet " "
3 Lemons,
1 gallon Bourbon Whisky.

Let the spirits remain on the ingredients 10 days, then strain it off, and add six pounds loaf sugar, and bottle.

ANTI SPASMODIC TINCTURE.

Cayenne pepper half an ounce, blood root 1 oz; epicac 2 oz, add these to one qt. alcohol and pint of water; let stand one week; a dose one tablespoonfull mixed with water. It is useful in inflamation of the lungs, pleurisy, whooping cough, consumption and difficult expectoration.

DROP BISCUIT.

Take three cups sweet milk and 6 cups flour, into which rub 4 tea spoonfuls cream tartar 1½ Sup. Carb. Soda, and pass the flour through a seive—mix with the batter ; add butter size of an egg, melted, and a little salt. Drop on tins to bake.

GINGER-BREAD.

1 cup molasses; 1 of each, sugar, butter, and sour milk, tea-spoon of each ginger, and cinnamon, ½ tea-spoon cloves, as much flour as can be stired in and make it very stiff.

PORTUGAL CAKE.

One ℔. flour, ¾ lb. sugar, ½ lb. of butter, eight eggs. one nutmeg, two spoonfuls lemon juice, 1 ℔. rasins.

SALLY'S JUMBLES.

Two coffee cups of Sugar,
One   "   "   Butter,
"   table spoon full Sour Milk,
a very little soda, 4 eggs, and a little seed.

CRULLERS.

1 cup sour milk, saleratus, ½ cup butter, 4 eggs, nutmeg and cinnamon.

LEMON CREAM.

Boil the rinds of 4 lemons in a quart of cream, squeeze and strain the juice of one lemon, sweeten it, and when the cream is cold stir it in.

QUINCE JELLY.

Cut your quinces in slices without pairing them, boil them in water, to each pint of liquid add 1 lb of sugar.

APPLE JELLY.

Boil a pail of sour apples with water enough to cover them, let them drain through a seive and to every pint of juice add 1 lb of sugar, lemon to your taste.

HARD WOFFLES.

½ lb butter, ½ lb sugar, 3 eggs, 3 tablespoons milk, a little nutmeg, flour to make it stiff enough.

LIQID OPEDELDOCK.

Take one quart of brandy and warm, then add 1 oz gum camphor, ¼ oz sal ammonia, ½ oz each of oil oreganum and rosemary, ¼ oz oil wormwood, when the oils are dissolved or mixed add six oz soft soap. This is excellent for Sprains and Bruises.

COCOANUT CAKE.

The whites of 16 or 17 eggs, 1 lb of sugar, ¾ of butter, 1 of flour, 1 cocoanut, take some flour from the pound to flour the cocoanut, add it just before going into the oven.

COMMON CRULLERS.

4 eggs, 2 tea-cups sugar, 1 of milk or cream, ½ cup butter, a little saleratus.

MUFFINS.

1 quart milk, 2 eggs, flour to make it about as thick as soft waffles, yeast sufficient to raise them: Just before baking stir in a little melted butter.

ICING FOR CAKES.

Beat the whites of eggs to an entire froth; to each egg, add 5 spoonfuls of sifted loaf-sugar; gradually beat it a great while. Put it on while your cake is hot, and set it in a warm oven to dry.

RHEUMATIC PLASTER.

Take one pound Resin, 4 ounces Sulphur, one ounce Camphor gum, ¼ ounce Cayenne Pepper. Put in a little neats foot oil or tallow and simmer them together; turn it into water and work it as you do wax.

CHINESE JELLY & HONEY.

Put into a pint of water the fourth of an ounce of alum; boil on a quick fire, then remove it; and stir in four pounds of White Sugar; boil on a quick fire for two minutes; set it off and let the boiling subside; replace it on the fire for a half minute, twice; strain it through a cotton cloth. When cool, add a teaspoonful of this to four pounds of Jelly. For Lemon Jelly, put one drop of Oil of Lemon in the bottom of the jar; pour the Jelly on it while warm, and let it stand for ten hours. Make different Jellies by using different Oils.

HONEY.—Put one fourth of a lb of pure honey in a jar, and four pounds of Jelly; let it stand for three hours. To prepare the extract, put one ounce of pulverized Jamaica Ginger and twenty drops Otto of Roses into a pint of pure alcohol, shake twice a day for two days.

LIP SALVE.

One ounce of white wax, two ounces of hog's lard, 1s. worth of the Balsam of Peru, a few raisins, shred very fine, and as much alkanet root as will color it. Dissolve all in a pipkin on the fire before you add the alkanet root; then strain it through muslin and put it into boxes for use.

FRENCH SOAP.

Take five lbs White Bar soap.
Take one half lb of salsoda.
Take one fourth lb of Borax.
And eighteen quarts of soft water.
Slice the soap fine, and boil until dissolved. Then dissolve the salsoda and borax in a little warm water, add while on the fire; let it boil three minutes and it is fit for use as soon as cold.

DIRECTIONS.—Soak the clothes in a little warm soap suds fifteen minutes, then rinse them out, put them in clean suds, and boil fifteen minutes, then rinse them out and hang up.

FOR MAKING HARD SOAP.—Add a half lb of white Resin and a little less water.

DOCT. WOOD'S HAIR TONIC.

Rose water 4 ounces, sugar lead 1 drachm; mix well together; the above will make two quarts by adding water.

LEMON MEAD.

8 gallons of water 8 lbs white sugar, one pint of good yeast, mix all together, flavor with lemon oil to suit the taste; put it in a jug, let it stand 12 hours, keep over night, then it is fit for use.

WASHING FLUID.

Take one pound of salsoda, and a half a pound of unslaked lime; put them in a gallon of water, and boil twenty minutes: let it stand till cool, then drain off, and put it away in a stone jug or jar. Soak your dirty clothes over night, or until they are well wet through; then wring them out and rub on plenty of soap, and to one boiler of clothes, well covered over with water, add one teacupful of the washing fluid. Boil half an hour briskly, then wash them thoroughly through one suds, and rinse well through two waters, and your clothes will look better than the old way of washing twice before boiling.

TO DRY PLUMS.

Split ripe plums, take the stones from them, and lay on plates or sieves to dry, in a warm oven or hot sun; take them in at sunset, and do not put them out again until the sun will be upon them; turn them that they may be done evenly; when perfectly dry, pack them in jars or boxes lined with paper, or keep them in bags; hang them in an airy place.

LONDON BUTTER SCOTCH.

10 lbs white sugar, 1 lb butter, $\frac{1}{4}$ oz. tartaric acid, $\frac{1}{4}$ oz. of Alum.

SUPERIOR WASHING SOAP.

Take 5 pounds white bar soap, three pounds sal soda, eight ounces Borax, put them into 20 qt*. soft water, heat and stir until dissolved then remove from the fire, add 2 oz. Carbonate of Ammonia. While hot stir the whole together, when cold it is fit for use.

A cheaper article may be made by substituting 7 lbs. of soft.soap instead of the hard soap.

SODA SYRUP.

1 oz. of tartaric acid, to 3 lbs of white sugar, 1 pint of water to every lb sugar, flavor with lemon oil to suit the taste, the whites of 3 eggs, to every 10 lbs sugar, mix all together let it come to a boil, strain through a flannel cloth or bag. This is the way to make all kinds of syrups for soda only; flavor with oil of lemon, sassafras, wintergreen, or what suits your taste.

LUCY'S RYE CAKES.

Four and a half cups rye meal, three eggs, one and a half tea-spoonfuls cream tartar, even teaspoonful soda; mix with milk to make as thick as pound cake. Bake in hearts and rounds. To be eaten hot, for breakfast or tea.

CALF'SFOOT JELLY.

4 Calf's feet, 4 qts. of water boil down to 2 let it cool, skim the grease off it, set it over the fire till dissolved, add 2 ozs. of isingglass, 1 lb of white sugar to 1 pint of the liquid, the white of 5 eggs beaten to a froth, cinnamon, mace or oil of lemon to suit the taste.

CALF'SFOOT JELLY.

3 ozs of jelliton, dissolved in 3 qts. of water, and one pint maderia wine, 3 lemons, 3 lbs white sugar, the whites of 4 eggs, beaten to a froth, boil it; strain in through a flannel cloth set it away until cold undisturbed.

MACAROONS.

1 lb of almonds made fine, the whites of 12 eggs, mixed in one at a time till they are all mixed with the almonds, then add 2 lbs of white sugar; bake them in a cool oven.

SUGAR CAKE.

8 lbs sugar, 24 eggs, 4 lbs butter, 2 qt. water, 4 ozs hartshorn, flour enough to make it work.

COMMON POUND CAKE.—5 lbs sugar, 3 lbs butter, 36 eggs, 3 ozs hartshorn, 3 pints water, 10 lbs flour.

BLUE-STOCKING PUDDING.

Two-thirds cup of butter, one cup molasses, two cups milk, two teaspoons saleratus, four eggs, two pounds raisins, stoned and chopped, a quarter pound citron, cloves, cinnamon, nutmeg and salt to taste; flour to make as thick as pound cake. Steam or boil five hours. To be eaten with wine sauce.

CORN MEAL PUDDING WITHOUT EGGS.

Take six table-spoonfuls of meal, and stir molasses enough to have the meal all wet, and no more; that will sweeten it enough: then take one quart of milk and boil it; pour it on the meal boiling hot; stir the meal while pouring the milk on to it, so as not to have it lumpy; stir in three table-spoonfuls of wheat flour, wet with a little cold milk; salt it, and bake two hours; add spices, if you like. This will make an excellent pudding.

QUEEN'S CAKE.

One pound flour, one pound sugar, three-quarters of a pound of butter, five eggs, one gill wine, one gill brandy, one gill cream, one nutmeg, one pound raisins. Simmer the wine, brandy, cream and spice together, and let it get quite cold before adding the rest.

TOMATO FIGS.

Pour boiling water over the tomatoes, in order to remove the skin; then weigh and place them in a stone jar, with as much sugar as you have tomatoes, and let them stand two days; then pour off the syrup, and boil and skim it until no skum rises. Then pour it over the tomatoes, and let them stand two days, as before; then boil and skim again. After the third time they are fit to dry, if the weather is good; if not, let them stand in the syrup until drying weather. Then place on large earthen plates or dishes, and put them in the sun to dry, which will take about a week, after which pack them down in small wooden boxes, with fine white sugar between every layer. Tomatoes prepared in this manner will keep for years.

TOMATO MEAT PIE.

Cover the bottom of a pudding-dish with bread crumbs; then make a layer of cold roasted mutton, cut in small pieces; then a layer of tomatoes, sliced; then another layer of bread crumbs, another of meat, another of tomatoes, and then cover with bread crumbs, and bake till the crust is brown. Season with salt and pepper to your tast. It will bear high seasoning. Serve hot, and a better relishing dish is not often met with.

TO PRESERVE PLUMS WITHOUT THE SKINS.

Pour boiling water over large egg or magnum bonum plums, cover them until it is cold, then pull off the skins. Make a syrup of a pound of sugar and a teacup of water for each pound of fruit; make it boiling hot, and pour it over; let them remain for a day or two, then strain it off and boil again; skim it clear, and pour it hot over the plums; let them remain until the next day, then put them over the fire in the syrup; boil them very gently until clear; take them from the syrup with a skimmer into the pots or jars; boil the syrup until rich and thick; take off and skum that may arise, then let cool and settle, and pour it over the plums. If brown sugar is used, which is quite as good, except for greengages clarify it as directed.

TOMATO KETCHUP.

One gallon of skinned tomatoes; four table spoonfuls of salt; four of black pepper; half tablespoonful of allspice; one of red pepper; three of mustard; three large onions cut fine; simmer all together with a pint of sharp vinegar for three or four hours; then strain through a wire sieve, and bottle close. Those who prefer it may add, when cool, two tablespoonfuls of juice of garlic.

3

PINE APPLE JELLY.

Pare and grate the pineapple, and put into the preserving pan with one pound of fine white sugar to every pound of fruit; stir it and boil until well mixed, and thicken sufficiently, then strain it, pour it into jars, and when it has become cool, cover the jellies with papers wet with brandy; cover the jars tightly, and treat them as apple jelly.

CURRANT AND RASPBERRY JELLY.

Pick over a quart of red currants, a quart of white currants, and a quart of raspberries; put the whole over the fire, stir them and boil them about ten minutes, then rub them through a sieve; strain the liquor, while hot, through a jelly bag, add a pound of fine white sugar to every pint of liquor; boil and treat it as directed for apple jelly.

TOMATO TART.

Cover a plate with a thin laying of dough. Cut your tomatoes (green) into thin slices, and place them on the dough, very evenly; then add two table-spoonfuls of brown sugar, and one of ground cinnamon. Spread them evenly over the tomato, and bake well. This makes a delicious tart. The tomatoes used should be sound and sweet.

MILK RISING BREAD.

This is made, altogether, in many families; especially in the country, where baker's yeast is not to be procured. It is a very white and beautiful bread when well-made, though hardly as nutritious as hop yeast. It is less trouble to make it than almost any other kind, after the housewife has once acquired the art. Take of milk, according to the size of the baking required, make it blood-warm by putting in hot water, about half in half; add salt in proportion of a teaspoonful to a pint; make a thin batter—not very thin—set the vessel containing it in a larger one, so that it will be surrounded with lukewarm water, which must be kept at that temperature until the sponge rises. It should be very light; but it must not stand too long, as it acquires a disagreeable odor, and makes wet, heavy bread by so doing. As soon as light, pour the sponge into the center of your baking of flour; add more milk or water; knead into loaves, set to rise in buttered pans, bake half or three quarters of an hour in rather a quick oven. This bread dries sooner than most other varieties, and should be made often.

SODA BISCUITS.

Measure out the exact quantity of flour which you will require, so that the proportions will be maintained : one quart of flour; one pint of water; one small teaspoonful of soda; two of cream tartar; two ounces of butter.   Rub the butter thoroughly into the flour ; after this is done, stir the cream of tartar equally through it; dissolve the soda in the water, which should be slightly warmed, pour it into the centre of the flour, mix it up lightly, hastily, and not too stiff, roll it out upon the moulding-board, cut them out with cake cutter or tumbler, place them upon floured pans, bake immediately in a quick oven.   Every cook can have soda biscuits of a quality to delight the palate by a little care in following these directions. All mixtures which are lightened with soda and cream of tartar should be so put together that the greater part of the fermentation will take place after they go into the oven. For this reason biscuits should not stand long after being made.   A quick oven is absolutely necessary to their proper baking ; it should be hot when they are placed in it. Twenty minutes is enough for them.   They should also be served shortly after they are baked.

Observe : cream of tartar is more apt to

vary in strength than soda. The usual proportions should be twice as much in bulk of cream of tartar, whatever the mixture in which it is placed. Should the dough, upon baking, have a greenish tinge, it is evident that the cream of tartar is deficient in quality—a little more must be used.

JOHNNY CAKE.

A quart of sour or butter milk; a little salt: a piece of butter half the size of an egg; corn-meal enough for a stiff batter. Just before placing upon buttered tins for the oven, add a heaped teaspoonful of soda or saleratus. An egg should be added if convenient. If a richer cake is desired, two eggs and a spoonful of syrup or sugar should be used. Bake three quarters of an hour.

APPLE JOHNNY CAKE.

Where rich, tender apples are plenty, such as are suitable for dumplings, three or four apples, pared and sliced into the batter, make a delicious variety of this kind of hot bread.

SODA BISCUIT CRACKERS.

Take to one bbl of flour, 3 pails water, 20 lbs lard, 10 oz. saleratus, 2½ lbs salt, 4 qt. Bakers' yeast.

BUCKWHEAT CAKES.

Stir buckwheat flour into lukewarm water; it will take nearly a quart of flour to a pint of water; add a small cup yeast. Set it to rise over night, if wished for breakfast. Leave plenty of room in the vessel containing it, or it will overrun. If it should be sour in the morning, add soda until it is sweet. These cakes should not stand, after baking, so as to sweat, as that destroys the crispness which should be a part of their excellence. They should be served when taken from the griddle. Use part of the last batter to rise the next, when you have them daily.

CORN GRIDDLE CAKES.

Make your batter of sour or butter-milk, and a little thicker than when wheat-flour is used. A handful of wheat flour should be stirred in, or they will break in pieces while being turned. Cakes, half of white flour half of corn-meal, are more easily digested than wheat alone.

TOMATO GRIDDLE CAKES.

Slice ripe tomatoes into a nice batter, and fry them. To lovers of that vegetable they are a delectable dish.

BANNOCK.

Two cups of meal; two of flour; a tea-spoonful of salt; one of ginger; four spoons-ful of molasses; wet with butter-milk or sour milk; a teaspoonful of saleratus. Bake an hour.

RICH GRIDDLE CAKES.

Griddle cakes are better to have about four eggs to a quart of milk. To be very nice, the eggs should be beaten separately. They can then be made with sweet milk, and a little soda and cream of tartar added.

WILLIE'S INDIAN CAKE.

One pint milk, one tea-spoonful saleratus, three eggs, one tea-spoonful salt, one table-spoonful flour, two eggs, Indian meal to make a *thin* batter. Bake three-quarters of an hour.

FRITTERS.

Make a stiff batter of flour in a quart of warm milk; add a gill of melted butter, a little salt, and three eggs well beaten; half a teaspoonful of soda, and a teaspoonful of cream tartar. Drop this mixture from a spoon, in pieces the size of an egg, into a kettle of hot lard, and fry them brown.

MUFFINS.

To a quart of warm milk add an egg, a piece of butter the size of a hen's egg, a little salt, and a gill of yeast: stir in flour to make a thick batter; let it stand to rise in a warm place, (if for breakfast, they can be set the night before); butter your rings, and put them upon a hot griddle well greased. When a good brown upon one side, turn them; do not burn them.

MUFFINS.

Very delicious muffins may be made, at a few moments' notice, by using four eggs to a quart of milk, and omitting the yeast. Stir in flour until a thick batter. The eggs should be beaten separately; a little more butter may be used. This kind will be nice baked in small tins in the oven, instead of in rings upon the griddle.

APPLE FRITTERS.

Slice tart, tender apples in thin pieces into the flour for the batter.

SWEET FRITTERS.

Put a teacupful of sugar into a quart of batter.

WAFFLES.

Make a thicker batter than for the griddle cakes, but not too thick. Allow at least two eggs to a quart of milk. Have your waffle-irons well-heated and greased ; fill one side ; shut them up ; keep both sides hot by turning.

CORN STARCH PIE.

To one quart of milk put two table-spoonfuls of corn starch, and two eggs. Sweeten, salt and season to the taste. Line a pie-plate with crust, and bake as custard.

FLOATING ISLAND.

One quart of milk, the yelks of three eggs, and table-spoonful of flour, stirred in the milk when boiling hot ; let it just boil ; then pour into your dish ; drop the beaten whites into hot water, and lay on the top when cool.

SAGO PUDDING.

Wash a teacupful of sago ; put in your pudding-dish, and pour on a quart of boiling water, stiring all the time ; put in a little salt, and a table-spoonful of sugar. The longer it stands thus before baking, the better. Bake slowly an hour. Eaten with sugar and butter stirred together,

SCRAMBLED EGGS.

Beat up a few eggs with a little salt, turn them into a pan which has in it a little melted butter, stir them until thickened, turn them out into a hot dish.

OMELETTE.

Beat up five eggs with a quart of milk, a little salt, and a teacup of flour; have your frying-pan at a very moderate heat, put about an ounce of butter in it; turn half the above quantity into it at once; let it do slowly, until it is of a light brown upon the under side and thickened throughout; with a broad knife turn half the omelette over upon the other half, so that it will be brown upon the outer sides; take it up carefully upon a warm plate, and serve immediately. Put another ounce of butter in the pan, and fry the remainder. Many persons like a little fine-chopped parsley in it; or parsley and about two ounces of cold-boiled ham chopped fine.

TO MAKE HARD WATER SOFT.

Take one oz. of fresh lime and stir it well in a bucket of water, then stir all thoroughly in a barrel of water, and as soon as it settles the water will be soft and fit for use, as it will drive every impurity to the bottom.

BEEF A LA MODE.

Cut the meat into pieces of three or four ounces each; mince a couple of onions and put them, with a quarter-pound of beef-dripping, into a large, deep stew-pan. As soon as it quite hot, flour the meat, put in the pan, keep stirring it; when it has been on about ten minutes, dredge it with flour until you have stirred in as much as will thicken; then cover it with boiling water, adding it gradually, and stirring it at the time (it will take two quarts to six pounds of meat); skim it when it boils; then put in one drachm of ground black pepper, two of allspice, and two bay cloves; set the pan by the fire, or at a distance over it; let it stew very slowly for two or three hours. When you find the meat sufficiently tender, put it into a tureen, and it is ready for the table.

PICKLE FOR CORNING BEEF.

For one hundred pounds beef, six gallons water; nine pounds salt, half coarse, half fine; three pounds brown sugar; one quart of molasses; three ounces of saltpetre. Boil it all together, skim off the scum, and after packing the beef in a tub or barrel, pour the hot contents over the meat. This partially cooks it, makes it tender, and keeps it sweet.

MINCED PIE.

Boil fresh beef perfectly tender, that will slip off the bone. The head and harslet are nice for this purpose. Take out all the hard gristle and bone and tough parts, when hot. As soon as it is cold, chop it all very fine, and if you do not want it for immediate use, season it with pepper, salt, cloves and cinnamon, and press it closely into a stone jar,and pour molasses over the top,and when after a few days or weeks, it has left the surface, pour on more to keep it nice. To every two quarts of chopped meat, a half a teacupful of ground-cinnamon, a table-spoonful of ground cloves, a teaspoonful of pep-, per, and a table-spoonful of salt, will keep it well, with molasses poured over it, a year. It is far more convenient to have meat thus prepared for use through the winter than to boil every time it is needed. The proportion should be a third meat, and two thirds apple, chopped very fine; those a little sour are best. A good mince-pie is a general favorite, and formerly, brandy was deemed indispensable in giving them the right flavor. But we are happy to inform our temperance friends and others, that a mince-pie can be made equally good without either wine or brandy. Add a good quantity of raisins, and season high with spices and molasses, adding water sufficient to keep them moist, made up in a rich nice paste, and there will be nothing wanting in flavor or quality. They should be baked one hour in a moderate oven.

VARNISH FOR PICTURES OR MAPS.

Take of Balsam of Fir one oz., spirits of Turpentine two ozs.—mix well together.

Before this composition is applied the picture or drawing must be sized with a solution of Ichthaocila, or fish glue. When dry apply the varnish.

LINIMENT.

Alcohol 1 qt., gum camphor 4 ozs., turpentine 2 ozs., oil origanum 2 ozs., sweet oil 1 oz. For cuts or corks in horses or cattle, (in winter,) it has no equal; work right along, but put it on often. For human flesh use twice the amount of alcohol, and no liniment will be found superior to it.

COUGH SYRUP.

Take syrup of squills 2 oz., tartarized antimony 8 grs., sulphate of morphine 5 grs., pulverized gum arabic ¼ oz., honey 1 oz., water 1 oz.—mix. Dose for an adult, small teaspoonful; repeat in half an hour if it does not relieve. Child in proportion.

ENGLISH DINNER WINE.

FROM GARDEN RHUBARB, OR PIE PLANT.

An agreeable and healthful wine is made from the expressed juice of the garden Rhubarb. To each gallon of juice add one gallon of soft water in which 7 pounds of brown sugar has been dissolved; fill a keg or barrel with this proportion, leaving the bung out, and keep it filled with sweetened water as it works off until clear. Any other vegetable extract may be added if this flavor is not liked, then bung down or bottle as you desire. These stalks will furnish about three-fourths their weight in juice. Fine and settle by dissolving isinglass in a small portion of the liquid, and pouring into the keg or barrel.

EYE WATER.

Take one table spoonful each of table salt and sulphate of zinc, (white vitriol,) burn it on copper or earthen until dry; $\frac{1}{2}$ pint soda water, a spoonful of white sugar, and sulphate of copper, (blue vitriol,) size of a pea. If too strong reduce with soft water. If the eyes are very sore, or of long standing, take a spoonful of epsom salts every other night for two or three times, and use three or four times daily of the eye-water.

FOR COACH PAINTING.

COACH LACCRE OR JAPAN.—One gallon of good Linseed oil, half pound shellac gum, half ℔ lithrage, half lb red lead. Make in an iron kettle over a coal fire. Heat gradually and continue stirring until all melted, then remove from the fire and add slowly a half ℔ sugar of lead. Reduce with three quarts spirits of turpentine when a little cool. Care must be taken to prevent burning while heating.

FOR FLOORS AND INSIDE HOUSE PAINTING.

Process of making same as Coach paint, above described. Use the following ingredients:

Seven quarts Linseed oil, half pound red lead, half pound lithrage, half pound gum shellac. Stir while making, and add while quite hot one gallon spirits of turpentine.

BEST BURNING FLUID.

Take nine pints of 95 or 98 per cent. alcohol and put in one quart of good camphene, and shake it briskly and it will become clear at once, when without the shaking it would take from six to seven quarts of alcohol to cut the camphene. This cannot be outdone.

GREEN MOUNTAIN SALVE.

FOR RHEUMATISM, BURNS, PAINS IN THE SIDE OR BACK, BOILS, &c.

Take 2 ℔s resin, ¼ lb burgundy pitch, ¼ ℔ beeswax, ¼ ℔ mutton tallow; melt them slowly. When not too warm, add 1 oz oil hemlock, 1 oz. balsam of fir, 1 oz. oil origanum, 1 oz. oil of red cedar, 1 oz. Venice turpentine, 1 oz. oil wormwood, ½ oz. verdigris. The verdigris must be very finely pulverised and mixed with the oils; then add as above, and work all in cold water as wax until cool enough to roll; rolls 5 inches long and 1 inch in diameter sell for 25 cts. This salve has no equal for rheumatic pains, or weakness in the side, back, shoulders, or any place where pain may locate itself. Where the skin is broken, as in ulcers, bruises, etc, omit the verdigris. This salve will be found a very superior and reliable article for all of the above specified purposes.

EXCELLENT HONEY.

Take five pounds good common sugar, 2 lbs. water; gradually bring to a boil, skimming well; when cool add one pound bees' honey, and four drops essence of peppermint. If you desire a better article use white sugar, a half pound less water and a half pound more honey.

JAVA HONEY.

Good brown sugar, 11 lbs.; water, 1 qt.; old bee bread honey in the comb, 2 pounds; cream tartar, 50 grs.; gum arabic, 1 oz.; oil of peppermint, 5 drops; oil of rose, 2 drops. Mix, and boil two or three minutes and remove from the fire. Have ready, strained, one quart of water in which a tablespoonful of pulverized slippery elm bark has stood sufficiently long to make it ropy and thick like honey. Mix this into the kettle with an egg well beaten up. Skim well in a few minutes, and when a little cool, add two pounds nice strained bees' honey and strain the whole, and you will have not only an article which looks and tastes like honey, but which possesses all its medicinal properties. It has been shipped in large quantities under the name of Java Honey. It will keep as fresh and nice as when made, any length of time if properly covered.

HONEY.

Take 5 lbs common brown sugar, 1 oz. cream tartar, 1½ pints water, 1½ lbs strained honey. Add a little water to the cream tartar to dissolve it, then stir all up together and boil and skim 15 or 20 minutes. This receipt is simple and reliable, and the honey will be found superior.

EXCELSIOR LINIMENT.
FOR IMMEDIATE RELIEF OF PAIN.

Take 95 per cent. alcohol, 2 qts., and add to it the following articles; oils of Hemlock and Sassafras, spirits of Turpentine, Balsam of Fir, chloroform, and tinctures of catechu and guaiaci (commonly called guac,) of each one oz.; oil of origanum, 2 ozs.; oil of wintergreen, ½ oz., and gum camphor, ½ oz.

DIRECTIONS FOR USE.—For Rheumatism, bathe the parts affected freely, and wet a piece of flannel and bind on the parts.

For Headache, Neuralgia, Cuts, Sprains, Burns, Bruises and Spinal Affections, bathe externally, immediately covering with dry flannel, or else wetting the flannel and keeping it on the part. If billious headache, take internally one teaspoonful in a little water every two hours, applying to the head at the same time until relief is obtained.

For Ear-ache, wet cotton or wool and put it into the ear. No article equals this for the ear.

For Tooth-ache, apply to the gum with the finger, and to the face over the painful teeth, pressing the hand on the face until it burns with heat.

For Sore Throat, take ten drops on sugar swallowing gradually, and bathe the throat freely. Repeat, in all cases, if necessary.

This receipt has been sold frequently for from ten to twenty-five dollars, and thousands of dollars have been made by agents manufacturing and selling the article.

DIARRHEA CORDIAL.

Best Rhubarb pulverized 1 oz., peppermint leaf pulverized 1 oz., capsicum ¼ oz., cover with boiling water and steep twenty minutes, strain through white woolens or filter, and add ½ oz. bi-carb. potash, ½ oz. essence cinnamon, and brandy (or good whisky,) equal in amount to the whole, and four ounces loaf sugar. Dose for an adult, one to two tablespoonsful; child, one to two teaspoonsful from three to six times per day or until relief is obtained.

TINCTURES.

Tinctures are made with 1 oz. of gum, root or bark, &c., dried, to each pint of proof spirit, and usually stand about one week and filter.

BARRELL'S INDIAN LINIMENT.

Alcohol, 1 qt.; tincture of capsicum, 1 oz; oils of origanum, sassafras, pennyroyal, hemlock, of each ½ ounce.—mix. This liniment is now kept for sale by most druggists, and has been in market 15 years.

RELIABLE TOOTH CORDIAL AND PAIN KILLER.

Alcohol, 95 per cent. 2 oz.; laudanum, ½ oz.; chloroform 1½ ozs.; gum camphor, 2 oz.; oil cloves, 2 drachms. Mix, and color with tincture of red sanders. If there is a nerve exposed this will quiet it. Apply with lint. Rub also on the gums and any place where there is pain.

VEGETABLE PHYSIC.

Jallap 1 oz., senna 2 oz., Peppermint 1 oz, (a little cinnamon if desired,) all pulverized and sifted through gauze. Dose, 1 tea spoonful put in a tea cup with two or three spoonsful of hot water and a good lump of loaf sugar; when cool drink all, to be taken fasting in the morning, drink gruel freely. If it does not operate in three hours repeat half the quantity.

GENUINE SEIDLITZ POWDER.

Rochelle salts 2 drachms; bi-carb. soda 2 scruples; put these into a blue paper, and put 35 grains of tartaric acid into a white paper. To use, put each into different tumbler, fill half with water and put a little loaf sugar in with the acid, then pour together and drink. This makes a very pleasant cathartic.

SALUDA BEER.

Take 30 gallons of water; brown sugar 20 lbs; ginger root brused 1 ¼ lbs.; cream tartar ¼ lb. ; carbonate of soda 3 oz. ; one teaspoonful of oil lemon cut in a little alcohol; whites of ten eggs well beat; hops 2 oz.; yeast 1 quart. The ginger root and hops should be boiled 20 or 30 minutes in enough of the water to make all milk warm, then strained into the rest and the yeast added and allowed to work itself clear as the cider and bottled.

ESSENCES.

Peppermint oil, 1 oz.; Alcohol, 1 pint, and the same proportion of any oil you wish to use. Peppermint is colored with tincture of turmeric, and cinnamon with tincture of red sandal or sanders wood. Wintergreen with tincture of kino. Most essences are only made half or quarter as strong, and are not worth buying.

☞ In getting up soda drinks, it will be found preferable to put about 4 oz. of carbonate, sometimes called super-carbonate of soda, into 1 pint of water and shake when you wish to make a glass of soda and pour of this into a glass until it foams well, instead of using dry soda.

TAPIOCA PUDDING.

To one pint of water, add a teacupful of tapioca, and soak over night. In the morning add two beaten eggs, three pints of milk, and bake as any other. Another: Half a pint of tapioca dissolved in a quart of milk while boiling; add six eggs when nearly cold, with nutmeg or cinnamon. Bake ten or fifteen minutes.

BOILING EGGS.

Time—two to four minutes. Two·minutes set about half the white of the egg, three minutes touch the yelk, and four minutes harden the whole egg. The clock should be watched, and the water kept at boiling point.

PUDDING WITHOUT MILK.

Crumble or cut bread fine, pour boiling water upon the bread, add salt and a little butter, two eggs beaten, and a tea-cup of English currants, or any other fruit to suit your taste.

BUTTER is improved by working the second time, after the lapse of twenty four hours, when the salt is dissolved, and the watery particles can be entirely removed.

BRITISH OIL.

This truly valuable remedy, for the cure of cuts, bruises, swellings and sores of almost every description, is made of the following ingredients: Take oils of Turpentine and Linseed each 8 oz.; oils of amber and juniper, each 4 oz; Barbadoes tar, three oz; Senaca oil, 2 oz.—mix.

SODA SYRUPS.

Loaf or crushed sugar 8 lbs.; pure water, 1 gallon, gum arabic, 1 oz.; mix in a brass or copper kettle; boil until the gum is dissolved, then skim and strain throug a white flannel, after which add tartaric acid $5\frac{1}{2}$ oz. dissolved in hot water; to flavor, use extract of lemon, orange, rose, pineapple, peach, sarsaparilla, strawberry, &c., $\frac{1}{2}$ an oz. or to your taste. If you use the juice of lemon and $1\frac{1}{2}$ lbs. of sugar to a pint, you do not need any tartaric acid with it; now use 2 or 3 tablespoonfuls of syrup, to $\frac{3}{4}$ of a tumbler of water and $\frac{1}{3}$ teaspoonful of super-carbonate of soda made fine; stir well and be ready to drink; the gum arabic, however, holds the carbonic acid so it will not fly off as rapid as common soda. For soda fountains 1 oz. of super-carbonate of soda is used to one gallon of water. For charged fountains no acids are needed in the syrup.

GINGER POP—NO. 1.

Take 5½ gallons water, ¾ lb. ginger root bruised, ½ oz. tartaric acid, 2¼ lbs. white sugar, whites of 3 eggs well beat, one small teaspoonful of lemon oil, 1 gill yeast; boil the root for thirty minutes in 1 gal. of the water, strain off, and put the oil in while hot, mix. Make over night; in the morning skim and bottle, keeping out sediments.

GINGER POP.

No 2.—Take 2 oz. best white jamaica ginger root (bruised,) water six quarts, boil 20 minutes, strain and add 1 oz. cream tartar, 1 lb. white sugar, put on the fire and stir until all the sugar is dissolved and put into an eathern jar, now put in ¼ oz. tartaric acid, and the rind of one lemon; let it stand until 70 deg. of Farenheit, or until you can bear your hand in it with comfort, then add 2 tablespoonfuls of yeast, stir well, bottle for use and tie the corks. Make a few days before it is wanted for use.

SUBSTITUTE FOR CREAM FOR COFFEE.

Beat up a fresh egg; then pour boiling water on it gradually, to prevent its curdling. It is difficult to distinguish it from rich cream.

TO CURE RING BONE.

One half pint of Alcohol, a half pint of sweet oil, a half pint spirits of turpentine, 2 oz. hartshorn in the spirits, 1 ounce of coperas, 1 oz. camphor gum. Pulverize the coperas, and mix well. Let the horse stand on the ground. Wash it once a day and bathe it in with a hot iron, for 15 days. This remedy may be relied on.

TO MAKE VINEGAR.

Add three quarts of molasses to eight quarts of clear rain water, in a good keg near the stove-pipe, put in two spoonsful of good yeast, or two dry yeast cakes. Shake it frequently. In about fifteen days put in a sheet of brown paper, cut in strips, which will create a mother.

SALVE FOR CHAPPED HANDS.

Take 1 oz. white wax; 1 oz. spermaceti; 2 oz. sweet oil. Simmered together.

BARBERS' SHAMPOON MIXTURE.

Half a pint of Alcohol, $\frac{1}{2}$ pt. rain-water, 1 tablespoonful hartshorn, 1 spoonful saleratus, 1 of sal soda. Pulverize the hartshorn and sodas, put all in a bottle and shake before using. The hair should be thoroughly rinsed with rain-water after using.

CHESEMAN'S ARABIAN BALSAM.

Take 1 oz. oil origanum, 1 oz. spirits of turpentine, 1 ounce rosemary, 1 oz. camphor gum and four pounds fresh butter. Put the four first-mentioned articles in a bottle, and shake them well together. Put the butter in an iron kettle and when melted mix the whole together. Then bottle it.

FOR SEASONING SAUSAGES.

To thirty pounds of meat add 11 oz. salt, 2½ oz. black pepper, 3 oz. sage, 2 oz. summer savory, 1 tea cup brown sugar, 2 teaspoons of salt petre, and 1 teaspoonful cayenne pepper.

YEAST.

Take a good single handful of hops, and boil for 20 minutes in 3 pints of water, strain, stir in a tea-cup full of flour, a tablespoonful of sugar and a teaspoonful of salt; when a little cool put in one gill brewers' or bakers' yeast; and after 4 or 5 hours cover up and stand in a cool place for use; make again from this unless you let it get sour.

BROWNING FOR GUN BARRELS.

Take 1 ounce spirits of wine, ½ oz. tincture of steel, 1 oz., spirits of nitre, ⅓ ounce blue vitriol. 1 pint of rain water.

VARIOUS WINES.

Take 38 gallons of good clarified cider, 1 gallon good brandy, 1 lb. crude tartar, (this is what is deposited by grape wines) 5 gallons of any wine you wish to represent, 1 pint of sweet milk to settle it; draw off in from 24 to 36 hours after thoroughly mixing.

BLACKBERRY AND STRAWBERRY WINES.

Are made by taking the above wine when made with port wine, and for every 10 gallons from 4 to 6 quarts of the fresh fruit brused and strained, or added and let stand till the flavor is extracted. More or less may be used to suit the taste. In bottling, 3 or 4 broken raising put into each bottle will add to their richness of flavor.

TO PRESERVE EGGS.

To 4 gallons water add 2 quarts fresh slaked lime and 2 quarts salt. Let stand 3 days before using and stir often.

Let your eggs down into a barrel filled with this mixture, with a dish, and they will settle down right end up with care, and keep for any reasonable length of time without any further care than to keep them covered with the fluid. Eggs may be laid down in this way any time after June.

LEMON, ORANGE AND RASPBERRY SYRUPS

Where you have lemons which are spoiling and drying up, take the insides which are yet sound, squeeze out the juice, and to each pint put 1 ½ lbs white sugar; add a little of the peel, boil a few minutes strain and cork for use. This will not require any acid but orange or raspberry; syrups are made in the same way with the addition of ¼ oz. of tartaric acid to each pint of juice, and ⅓ teaspoonful of soda to ¾ of a glass of water, with three or four tablespoonfuls of syrup. If water is added the syrup will not keep as well.

TURKISH CREAM NECTAR.

Part first. Take 1 gallon water, 6 lbs. loaf sugar, 6 oz. tartaric acid, gum arabic 1 oz. Part second. 4 teaspoonfuls of flour, the whites of four eggs, beat the flour and and eggs finely together, then add ½ pint water; when the first part is blood warm put in the second, boil three minutes and it is done. Directions: 3 tablespoonfuls of the syrup to a glass half or two-thirds full of water, and add ⅓ teaspoonful of super-carbonate of soda made fine; stir well and drink at your leisure. .

GINGER WINE.

Put one oz. good ginger root (bruised) in one qt. of ninty-five per cent alcohol, let it stand six days and strain, add four qts. water and one lb white sugar dissolved in hot water.

TO CURE BURNS.

Lime water and sweet oil of equal quantities, applied with a feather, will stop all pain.

WATER PROOF OIL BLACKING

Take one pint of camphene and put into it all the india rubber it will dissolve, 1 pint curriers oil, 6 pounds tallow, and 2 oz. lampblack, mix thoroughly, by heat. This is a nice thing for old harness and carriage tops, as well as for boots and shoes.

COLOGNE.

Take of oil rosemary, of lemon, each $\frac{1}{4}$ oz. oil of bergamot, oil of lavender, each $\frac{1}{8}$ oz., oil of cinnamon 8 drops, oils clove and rose each fifteen drops, best alcohol, 2 quarts, mix and shake well 2 or 3 times a day for a week. This will be better if deodorised or cologne alcohol is used.

CIDER WITHOUT APPLES.

To each gallon of cold water, put 1 ℔. common sugar, ½ oz. Tartaric Acid, 1 table-spoonful of yeast, shake well, make in the evening, and it will be fit for use next day. Make in a keg a few gallons at a time, lea-ving a few quarts to make into next time—not using yeast again until the keg needs rinsing. If it gets a little sour make more into it, or put as much water with it as there is cider, and put with the vinegar. If it is desired to bottle this cider by *manu-facturers of small drinks*, you will proceed as follows: Put in a barrel 5 gallons of hot water, 30 lbs. brown sugar, ¾ lb. tartaric acid, 25 gallons cold water, 3 pints of hop or brewers yeast, worked into a paste with ¾ lb. flour, and one pint of water will be re-quired in making this paste, put altogether in a barrel, which it will fill, and let it work 24 hours—the yeast running out of the bung all the time, by putting in a little occasion-ally to keep it full. Then bottle, putting in 2 or 3 broken raisins to each bottle, and it will nearly equal Champagne.

FOR MAKING ONE GALLON WASHING FLUID.

Four ounces salts of tarter, 4 oz. saleratus, 1 oz. salt petre, dissolved in pure rain water. This receipt has been sold for six dollars.

RAISIN WINE.

Take 3 lbs nice raisins, free of stems, cut each one in 2 or 3 pieces, put them into a stone jug with one gallon of pure soft water, let them stand two weeks uncorked, shaking occasionally, (warm place in winter;) strain through three or four thicknesses of wollen or filter, color with burned sugar, bottle and cork well for use. For saloon purposes add 1 pint good brandy. The more raisins that are used the better will be the wine, not exceeding 5 lbs.

SPRUCE BEER.

Take 3 gallons water, 1 quart and $\frac{1}{2}$ pint molasses, 3 eggs well beat, 1 gill yeast; into 2 quarts of the water boiling hot, put 50 drops of any oil you wish the flavor of; or mix 1 oz. each oil, sassafras, spruce and wintergreen, then use the 50 drops. For ginger flavor, take 2 oz. ginger root bruised, and a few hops, and boil 30 minutes in one gallon of water; strain and mix all. Let it stand two hours and bottle, using yeast of course as before.

FOR HOT DROPS, NO. 6.

To 2 qts. first rate brandy add $\frac{1}{2}$ ℔ gum myrrh, and 1 oz. African pepper.

TO REMOVE WARTS AND CORNS.

Those who have not the patience to follow the more reasonable cure for warts or corns, will pursue the following course with success, avoiding, however, the taking cold after removing the wart or corn. Take the potash paste, composed of 1 lb potash dissolved in ½ pt. water. Add half an oz. extract of balladona, and 1 oz. gum arabic, dissolved in a little water. Worked into a paste with wheat flour.

After having paired off the dead part of the wart or corn, put on the paste and let it remain from 5 to 8 minutes, when you will work around with a sharp knife and lift them out. Apply sweet oil or vinegar to kill the alkali.

CHOLERA MEDICINE.

Laudanum 2 drachms, spirits of camphor 1 drachm, sweet tincture of rhubarb 4 do., aqua ammonia, ½ do., oil peppermint fifteen drops. Dose, for adult half to one teaspoonful.

ANOTHER.—One oz. gum camphor, 1 oz. of laudanum, 4 oz. spirits of lavender, ½ pt. alcohol. Mix alcohol and camphor first. Dose from half to one teaspoonful once in two hours.

CURE FOR CONSUMPTION,
FROM AN OLD INDIAN DOCTOR.

Take 2 ℔s Dandelion root; 1 ℔ Spignard root; 1 ℔ Sarsaparilla; 1 ℔ Wintergreen leaves; 1 ℔ Princess Pine leaves; 2 ℔s Raisins; ½ ℔ Cinnamon; ½ ℔ Cloves; 2 lbs Hoarhound.

Boil the above ingredients in sufficient water to get out the strength, boil down to one gallon, strain and add 2 ℔s loaf sugar. Dose according to age and constitution from a half teaspoonful to a large tablespoonful, two or three times a day.

TOOTHACHE.

Take either Creosote, Oil of Cloves, Laudanum, or a mixture of powdered salt and alum moistened, put with a bit of cotton in the cavity of the tooth will stop the pain.

For ague in the face put on a hot poultice of hops or ginger on a piece of brown paper.

CHEAP AND VALUABLE LINIMENT FOR MAN OR BEAST.

Beat up one egg, and add 1 wine-glass of Turpentine, 1 wine-glass Vinegar, and one wine-glass Whisky. Put in one after another as above.

5

DOCTOR KITRIDGES
NERVE AND BONE LINIMENT.
Take beef's gall 1 qt. alcohol 1 pint volatile liniment 1 ℔. extra, turpentine 1 ℔., oil orriganum 4 oz., aqua ammonia 4 oz., tincture of cayenne ½ pint, oil of amber 3 oz., tincture of spanish flies 6 oz., mixed well.

Dr. SLOAN'S HORSE LINIMENT.
Resin 4 oz., bees wax 4 oz., lard 8 oz., honey 2 oz., melt and stir altogether over a slow fire and gently bring to a boil, as it begins to boil, slowly add ¾ pint spirits turpentine stiring all the time, remove from fire, stir till cool; good for horse flesh, hoof broken, galled back, cracked heels &c. &c.

Nothing is better for burns, scalds, on human flesh.

CURE FOR DYSENTERY.
Take Laudanum ½ oz., tincture of Kino 1 oz., Morphine 4 grains. Mix. Dose one teaspoonful 3 or 4 times a day.

SPRUCE BEER.
One oz. Spruce oil, one oz. oil Cloves, one oz. oil Sassafras, one oz. oil Wintergreen, one pint alcohol with yeast, molasses and water.

TO MAKE GOOD VINEGAR
IN THREE DAYS WITHOUT DRUGS.

Take three casks, and place them upon each other on end. The centre cask must be filled with cobs or shavings which have been previously soaked in good sharp vinegar, and air allowed to circulate through it by means of a few inch holes bored around the cask above the faucet which conducts the vinegar into the lower cask. A small opening must be left between the centre and top casks to permit the circulation of air. The bottom of the top cask must be pierced with small holes, having several bits of twine hanging from them, to conduct the vinegar evenly upon the cobs in the centre barrel.

When thus arranged take, if whisky is used, one gallon of whisky to every four gallons of water, and add ½ ℔ sugar. If cider is used put in one part cider and three parts water. To this add 1 pt. good yeast to each barrel vinegar, and have the the holes and twine so arranged that it will run through every 12 hours—returning the fluid to the top cask every night and morning, and in three days you will have good substantial vinegar which will keep, and also improve by age. The cobs will serve for use during the whole season.

HOP YEAST.

Boil a handful of hops in two quarts of water, till reduced to three pints, Then strain the liquor, and put it back in the pot, and thicken it with a cup of wheat flour, previously mixed smooth with a little cold water. Let it boil three or four minutes, then mix it with about six medium-sized potatoes, that have just been boiled, peeled, and mashed; let the whole stand until luke-warm, then strain it, and put to it a cup of good yeast, and set it where it will keep just lukewarm. When of a frothy appear-ance, add a table spoonful of salt. Turn it immediately into a jar, keep it covered up, and set it in a cool place. The potatoes may be omitted in making the yeast, but the yeast will not be so lively, nor the bread so delicate. Scald your yeast jar thoroughly, before putting in fresh yeast. If your yeast gets sour, on using it, put a tea spoonful of saleratus in, before mixing it with your bread. If it does not foam up well, it is too stale to use. This kind of yeast will keep well for a fortnight, excepting in quite hot weather. Yeast cakes are the best to use in summer, as they will keep well for a long time.

This yeast will be found excellent to use in the various beer receipts.

WEIGHTS AND MEASURES.

The following are established weights of various produce, and the rates by which they should be bought and sold :

A bushel of wheat 60 pounds ;

Shelled corn 56 lbs.;	Corn on cob 70 lbs. ;
Rye, 56 lbs. ;	Oats, 35 lbs. ;
Potatoes, 60 lbs. ;	Beans, 60 lbs. ;
Bran, 20 lbs.;	Clover seed, 62 lbs.;
Timothy seed 62 lbs.;	Flaxseed, 56 lbs. ;
Hemp seed 44 lbs. ;	Buckwheat, 52 lbs. ;
Blue-grass seed, 14 lbs.	Castor beans 46 lbs.;
Dried peaches, 33 lbs.	Dried apples, 24 lbs.;

UNEXPLOSIVE BURNING FLUID.

Take one quart Alcohol, 4 oz. of Ether, one half pint of refined Turpentine, Put them all into a jug or bottle together and shake up well. Let stand two or three days when it will be fit for use.

DEAD SHOT FOR BEDBUGS.

Corrosive sublimate, 1 oz.; muriatic acid, 2 ozs. ; water, 4 oz. Dissolve ; then add turpentine, 1 pint ; decoction of tobacco, 1 pint.-- Mix. For the decoction of tobaco, boil two oz. of tobacco in a pint of water. The mixture must be applied with a paint-brush. This wash is a *deadly poison*.

CONTENTS.

ERRATA.

Page 2, eighth line from bottom, read "16" instead of "3 tablespoonfuls."